# Conversational Recorder

## Student Book

# *Conversational Recorder*

## Student Book

*By*

## John M. Feierabend
## Rachel Grimsby

GIA Publications, Inc.

Chicago

*Conversational Recorder*
is available in the following editions and packages:

G-9033T
Teacher's Manual

G-9033S
Student Book with Recordings and Digital Access

G-9033D
Digital Access Only version: Student Book with Recordings

G-9033
Package: Teacher's Manual plus Conversational Recorder Student Book

G-9033C15
Class Set for 15 Students: Teacher's Manual plus 15 Student Books

G-9033C20
Class Set for 20 Students: Teacher's Manual plus 20 Student Books

Conversational Recorder
Student Book

John M. Feierabend
Rachel Grimsby

G-9033S
ISBN: 978-1-62277-394-7

Copyright © 2021 GIA Publications, Inc.
7404 South Mason Avenue, Chicago, IL 60638
www.giamusic.com

# Table of Contents

# *Introduction*

## Welcome to Conversational Recorder *by* John Feierabend

Welcome to a new approach for learning how to play the recorder! This book will guide you to learn by ear first using rhythm syllables and solfege syllables. Then you will learn how to read music notation. Each of the thirteen units presents a new rhythm or melody challenge. Steps 1–5 in each unit are designed for you to learn by ear. Steps 6–8 use notation to deepen your understanding through reading (eye learning). A three-step instrumental procedure is used throughout the book:

1. Sing
2. Sing and finger
3. Play

Two hundred online audio tracks are provided to help you practice the three-step instrumental procedure while learning the recorder at Steps 1–5. They may be accessed using the link below:

**www.giamusic.com/CRaudio**

*Always* sing examples before using the recorder. *Always* "sing and finger" before "playing." *Always* complete Steps 1–5 in each unit before studying Steps 6–8.

## Background of the Recorder *by* Rachel Grimsby

Likely the oldest example of a woodwind instrument, the recorders played by today's elementary students are not at all similar to the ancient instrument they resemble. The earliest examples of recorders found were made of bone, not wood, over two thousand years ago! The length of the instrument and the number of finger holes also varied between these ancient recorders. During the Renaissance and Baroque periods, the construction of recorders became standardized to resemble the recorders students across the world play today. These recorders were typically made from a single block of wood with a whistle-like (duct) mouthpiece, mostly a cylindrical bore and seven finger holes (six in front, with the thumbhole in the back). Today, recorders may be built from a single piece of wood or may come as a two- or three-piece instrument consisting of a head joint and body, or a head joint, foot joint, and body. Recorders made for use by elementary students are made of a high-quality plastic and, like their wooden counterparts, may come in one, two, or three pieces.

## How to Use This Book *by* **John Feierabend**

There are thirteen units in this book. Each unit begins with aural activities. Complete the aural activities before looking at the notation for that unit. The aural activities are provided online and can be found using the link provided in your recorder book. Notated examples are provided in the recorder book. Familiar patterns and songs are presented first and then followed by unfamiliar patterns and songs.

# UNIT 1

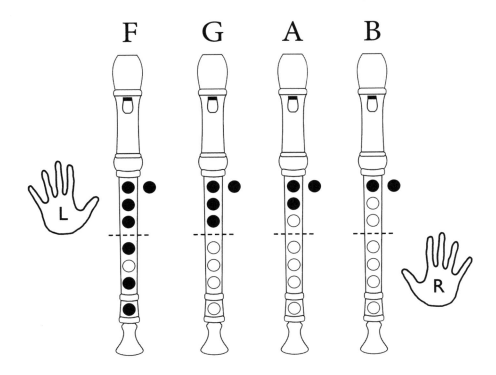

# Guided Practice Activities
## Unit 1

| | G = do | F = do |
|---|---|---|
| Step 2: Conversational Solfege–Rote: Patterns 1A | ____Track 1 | ____Track 5 |
| Step 3: Conversational Solfege–Decode/Familiar: Patterns 1A | ____Track 2 | ____Track 6 |
| Step 4: Conversational Solfege–Decode/Unfamiliar: Patterns 1B | ____Track 3 | ____Track 7 |
| Step 5: Conversational Solfege–Create | ____Track 4 | ____Track 8 |

*Complete all steps on this checklist with the voice first followed by recorder. Then proceed to the next page.*

# Patterns Set 1A

① Repeat each pattern after the teacher reads it aloud, or listen to the track and follow the directions. (Key of G: Track 1; Key of F: Track 5)

② Think and then speak each pattern using rhythm syllables.

③ Think and then play each pattern on any pitch.

# Patterns Set 1B

① Think and then speak each pattern using rhythm syllables.

② Think and then play each pattern on any pitch.

# UNIT 2

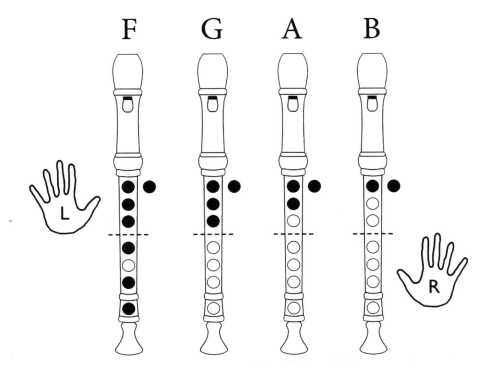

# Guided Practice Activities
## Unit 2

|  | G = do | F = do |
|---|---|---|
| Step 2: Conversational Solfege–Rote: Patterns 2A | _____Track 9 | _____Track 13 |
| Step 3: Conversational Solfege–Decode/Familiar: Patterns 2A | _____Track 10 | _____Track 14 |
| Step 4: Conversational Solfege–Decode/Unfamiliar: Patterns 2B | _____Track 11 | _____Track 15 |
| Step 5: Conversational Solfege–Create | _____Track 12 | _____Track 16 |

*Complete all steps on this checklist with the voice first followed by recorder. Then proceed to the next page.*

# Patterns Set 2A

① Repeat each pattern after the teacher reads it aloud, or listen to the track and follow the directions.
(Key of G: Track 9; Key of F: Track 13)

② Think and then speak each pattern using rhythm syllables.

③ Think and then play each pattern on any pitch.

# Patterns Set 2B

1. $\frac{6}{8}$ ♩. ♩. | ♩. ♩. |

2. $\frac{6}{8}$ ♪♪♪ ♪♪♪ | ♪♪♪ ♪♪♪ |

3. $\frac{6}{8}$ ♫♪ ♩. | ♩. ♫♪ |

4. $\frac{6}{8}$ ♪. ♪. | ♪. ♪♪♪ |

5. $\frac{6}{8}$ ♫♪ ♩. | ♫♪ ♫♪ |

6. $\frac{6}{8}$ ♪. ♪♪♪ | ♪♪♪ ♪♪♪ |

7. $\frac{6}{8}$ ♩. ♩. | ♫♪ ♫♪ |

8. $\frac{6}{8}$ ♪♪♪ ♪♪♪ | ♪. ♪♪♪ |

① Think and then speak each pattern using rhythm syllables.

② Think and then play each pattern on any pitch.

# UNIT 3

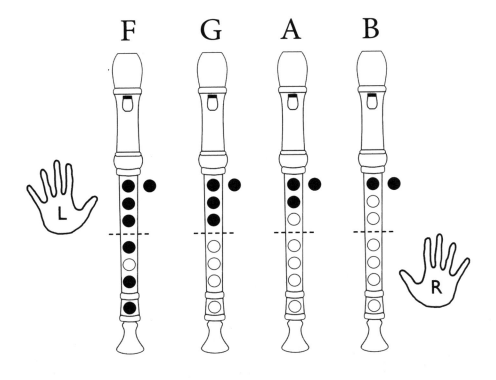

# *Guided Practice Activities*
## *Unit 3*

|  | G = do | F = do |
|---|---|---|
| Step 2: Conversational Solfege–Rote: Patterns 3A | ____Track 17 | ____Track 21 |
| Step 3: Conversational Solfege–Decode/Familiar: Patterns 3A | ____Track 18 | ____Track 22 |
| Step 4: Conversational Solfege–Decode/Unfamiliar: Patterns 3B | ____Track 19 | ____Track 23 |
| Step 5: Conversational Solfege–Create | ____Track 20 | ____Track 24 |

*Complete all steps on this checklist with the voice first followed by recorder. Then proceed to the next page.*

# Patterns Set 3A

① Repeat each pattern after the teacher reads it aloud, or listen to the track and follow the directions.
(Key of G: Track 17; Key of F: Track 21)

② Think and then speak each pattern using rhythm syllables.

③ Think and then play each pattern on any pitch.

# Patterns Set 3B

① Think and then speak each pattern using rhythm syllables.

② Think and then play each pattern on any pitch.

# UNIT 4

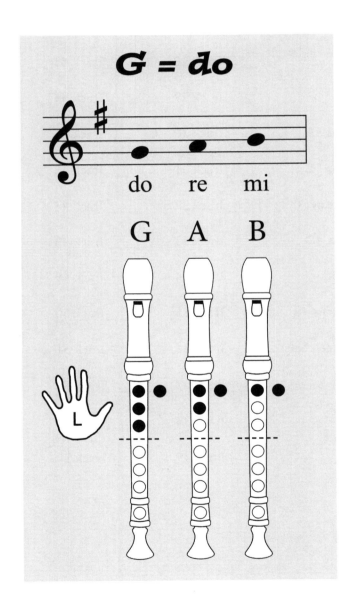

# *Guided Practice Activities*
## *Unit 4*

| | *G = do* | *F = do* |
|---|---|---|
| Step 1: Readiness–Rote: Closet Key | \_\_\_\_Track 25 | \_\_\_\_Track 40 |
| Step 1: Readiness–Rote: Fais Dodo | \_\_\_\_Track 26 | \_\_\_\_Track 41 |
| Step 2: Conversational Solfege–Rote: Patterns 4A | \_\_\_\_Track 27 | \_\_\_\_Track 42 |
| Step 2: Conversational Solfege–Rote: Patterns 4C | \_\_\_\_Track 28 | \_\_\_\_Track 43 |
| Step 2: Conversational Solfege–Rote: Patterns 4D | \_\_\_\_Track 29 | \_\_\_\_Track 44 |
| Step 3: Conversational Solfege–Decode/Familiar: Patterns 4A | \_\_\_\_Track 30 | \_\_\_\_Track 45 |
| Step 3: Conversational Solfege–Decode/Familiar: Patterns 4C | \_\_\_\_Track 31 | \_\_\_\_Track 46 |
| Step 3: Conversational Solfege–Decode/Familiar: Closet Key | \_\_\_\_Track 32 | \_\_\_\_Track 47 |
| Step 3: Conversational Solfege–Decode/Familiar: Patterns 4D | \_\_\_\_Track 33 | \_\_\_\_Track 48 |
| Step 3: Conversational Solfege–Decode/Familiar: Fais Dodo | \_\_\_\_Track 34 | \_\_\_\_Track 49 |
| Step 4: Conversational Solfege–Decode/Unfamiliar: Patterns 4B | \_\_\_\_Track 35 | \_\_\_\_Track 50 |
| Step 4: Conversational Solfege–Decode/Unfamiliar: Shoheen Sho | \_\_\_\_Track 36 | \_\_\_\_Track 51 |
| Step 4: Conversational Solfege–Decode/Unfamiliar: Sailor, Sailor | \_\_\_\_Track 37 | \_\_\_\_Track 52 |
| Step 5: Conversational Solfege–Create: Patterns in 2/4 | \_\_\_\_Track 38 | \_\_\_\_Track 53 |
| Step 5: Conversational Solfege–Create: Patterns in 6/8 | \_\_\_\_Track 39 | \_\_\_\_Track 54 |

*Complete all steps on this checklist with the voice first followed by recorder. Then proceed to the next page.*

# Patterns Set 4A

| G = do | F = do |
|---|---|
| 1.  | 1.  |
| 2.  | 2.  |
| 3.  | 3.  |
| 4.  | 4.  |
| 5.  | 5.  |
| 6.  | 6.  |
| 7. | 7.  |
| 8. | 8.  |

① Repeat each pattern after the teacher reads it aloud, or listen to the track and follow the directions.
   (Key of G: Track 27; Key of F: Track 42)

② Think and then sing each pattern using solfege syllables.

③ Think and then sing each pattern using solfege syllables while fingering.

④ Think and then play each pattern.

24

# *Patterns Set 4C*

① Repeat each pattern after the teacher reads it aloud, or listen to the track and follow the directions.
(Key of G: Track 28; Key of F: Track 43)

② Think and then sing each pattern using solfege syllables.

③ Think and then sing each pattern using solfege syllables while fingering.

④ Think and then play each pattern.

# Familiar Songs

## G = do

### 1. Closet Key

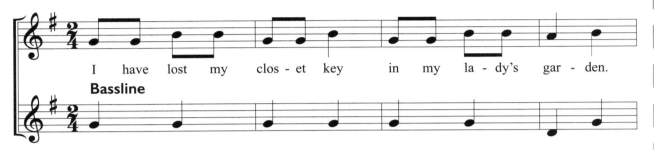

I have lost my clos - et key in my la - dy's gar - den.

**Bassline**

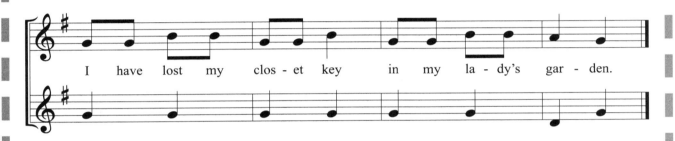

I have lost my clos - et key in my la - dy's gar - den.

### 2. Shoheen Sho

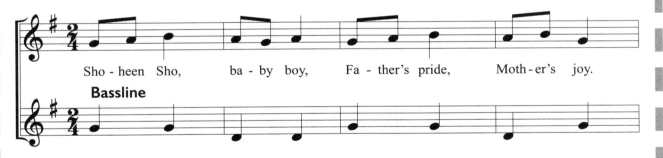

Sho - heen Sho, ba - by boy, Fa - ther's pride, Moth - er's joy.

**Bassline**

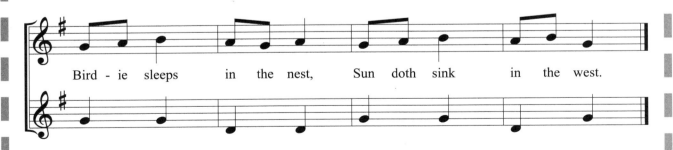

Bird - ie sleeps in the nest, Sun doth sink in the west.

# *Familiar Songs*

## *F = do*

### 3. **Closet Key**

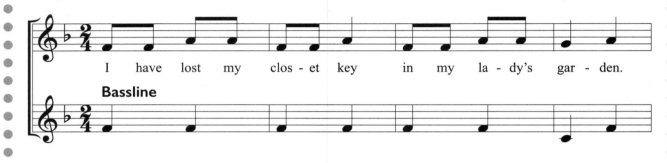

I have lost my clos-et key in my la-dy's gar-den.

**Bassline**

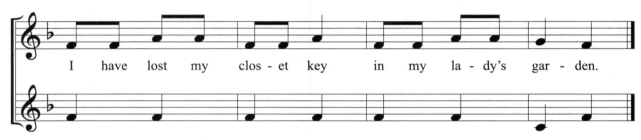

I have lost my clos-et key in my la-dy's gar-den.

### 4. **Shoheen Sho**

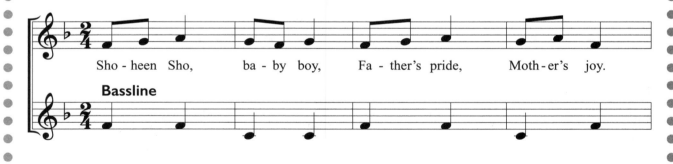

Sho-heen Sho, ba-by boy, Fa-ther's pride, Moth-er's joy.

**Bassline**

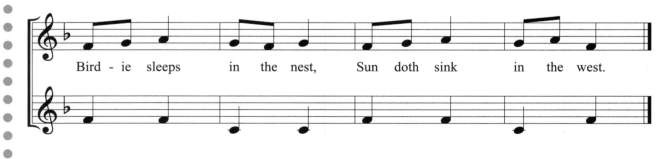

Bird-ie sleeps in the nest, Sun doth sink in the west.

# Patterns Set 4D

## G = do

## F = do

① Repeat each pattern after the teacher reads it aloud, or listen to the track and follow the directions.
(Key of G: Track 29; Key of F: Track 44)

② Think and then sing each pattern using solfege syllables.

③ Think and then sing each pattern using solfege syllables while fingering.

④ Think and then play each pattern.

# *Familiar Songs*

## *G = do*

### 5. Fais Dodo

Cajun

Fais do-do, Co-las mon p'tit frè-re, Fais do-do, t'au-ras du lo-lo.
Fais do-do, and let us go dream-ing, Fais do-do, come dream-ing with me.

**Bassline**

### 6. Sailor, Sailor

Sail-or, sail-or on the sea, Sail-or, sail-or on the sea,

**Bassline**

Sail-or, sail-or on the sea, What treas-ures have you brought for me?

# *Familiar Songs*

## *F = do*

### 7. **Fais Dodo**

Cajun

*Fais do-do, Co - las mon p'tit frè - re, Fais do-do, t'au - ras du lo - lo.*
Fais do-do, and let us go dream-ing, Fais do-do, come dream-ing with me.

**Bassline**

### 8. **Sailor, Sailor**

Sail - or, sail - or on the sea, Sail - or, sail - or on the sea,

**Bassline**

Sail - or, sail - or on the sea, What treas - ures have you brought for me?

# Patterns Set 4B

① Think and then sing each pattern using solfege syllables.

② Think and then sing each pattern using solfege syllables while fingering.

③ Think and then play each pattern.

# Unfamiliar Songs

## G = do

### 9. Snail Snail

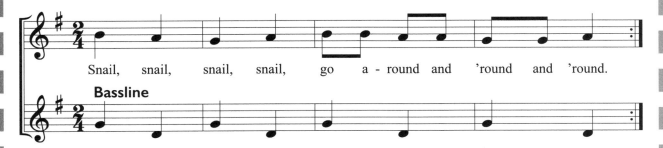

Snail, snail, snail, snail, go a-round and 'round and 'round.

**Bassline**

### 10. There She Goes

There she goes, there she goes, All dressed up in her Sun-day clothes.

**Bassline**

### 11. Long-Legged Sailor

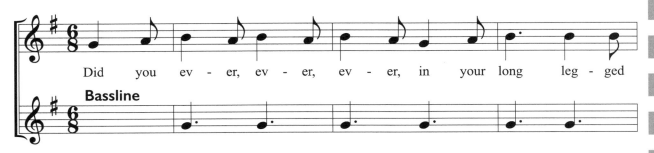

Did you ev-er, ev-er, ev-er, in your long leg-ged

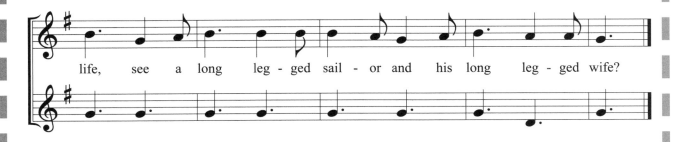

life, see a long leg-ged sail-or and his long leg-ged wife?

**Bassline**

# Unfamiliar Songs

## G = do (continued)

### 12. I'm a Little Dutch Girl

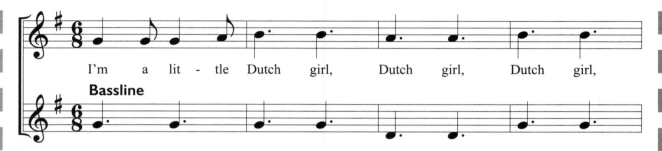

# *Unfamiliar Songs*

## *F = do*

### *13. Snail Snail*

Snail, snail, snail, snail, go a - round and 'round and 'round.

**Bassline**

### *14. There She Goes*

There she goes, there she goes, All dressed up in her Sun - day clothes.

**Bassline**

### *15. Long-Legged Sailor*

Did you ev - er, ev - er, ev - er, in your long leg - ged

**Bassline**

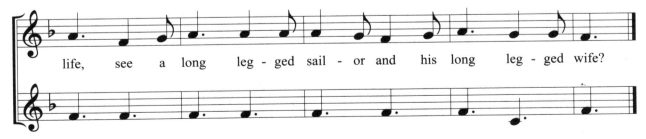

life, see a long leg - ged sail - or and his long leg - ged wife?

# Unfamiliar Songs

## F = do (continued)

### 16.  I'm a Little Dutch Girl

# UNIT 5

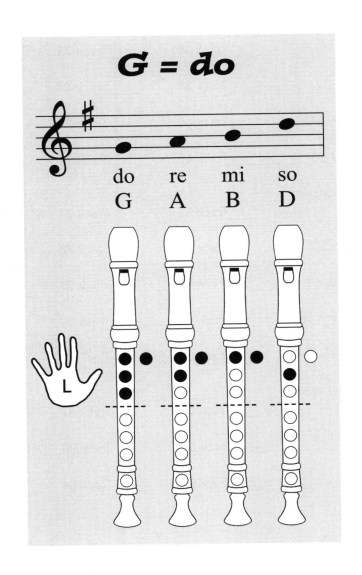

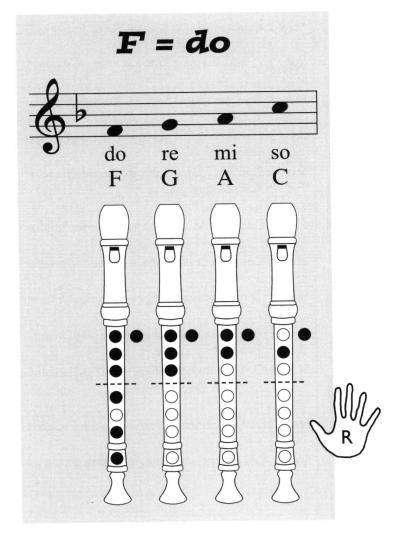

# *Guided Practice Activities*
## *Unit 5*

|  | G = do | F = do |
|---|---|---|
| Step 1: Readiness–Rote: Let Us Chase the Squirrel | _____Track 55 | _____Track 70 |
| Step 1: Readiness–Rote: Knock at the Door | _____Track 56 | _____Track 71 |
| Step 2: Conversational Solfege–Rote: Patterns 5A | _____Track 57 | _____Track 72 |
| Step 2: Conversational Solfege–Rote: Patterns 5C | _____Track 58 | _____Track 73 |
| Step 2: Conversational Solfege–Rote: Patterns 5D | _____Track 59 | _____Track 74 |
| Step 3: Conversational Solfege–Decode/Familiar: Patterns 5A | _____Track 60 | _____Track 75 |
| Step 3: Conversational Solfege–Decode/Familiar: Patterns 5C | _____Track 61 | _____Track 76 |
| Step 3: Conversational Solfege–Decode/Familiar: Let Us Chase the Squirrel | _____Track 62 | _____Track 77 |
| Step 3: Conversational Solfege–Decode/Familiar: Patterns 5D | _____Track 63 | _____Track 78 |
| Step 3: Conversational Solfege–Decode/Familiar: Knock at the Door | _____Track 64 | _____Track 79 |
| Step 4: Conversational Solfege–Decode/Unfamiliar: Patterns 5B | _____Track 65 | _____Track 80 |
| Step 4: Conversational Solfege–Decode/Unfamiliar: I Have a Dog | _____Track 66 | _____Track 81 |
| Step 4: Conversational Solfege–Decode/Unfamiliar: Johnny Works With One Hammer | _____Track 67 | _____Track 82 |
| Step 5: Conversational Solfege–Create: Patterns in 2/4 | _____Track 68 | _____Track 83 |
| Step 5: Conversational Solfege–Create: Patterns in 6/8 | _____Track 69 | _____Track 84 |

*Complete all steps on this checklist with the voice first followed by recorder. Then proceed to the next page.*

# Patterns Set 5A

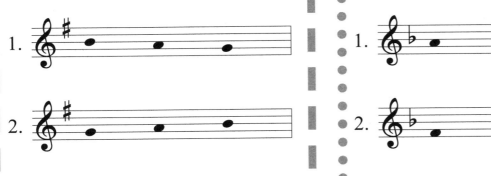

**G = do**

1.

2.

3.

4.

5.

6.

7.

8.

**F = do**

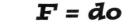

1.

2.

3.

4.

5.

6.

7.

8.

① Repeat each pattern after the teacher reads it aloud, or listen to the track and follow the directions.
(Key of G: Track 57; Key of F: Track 72)

② Think and then sing each pattern using solfege syllables.

③ Think and then sing each pattern using solfege syllables while fingering.

④ Think and then play each pattern.

38

# Patterns Set 5C

## G = do

## F = do

① Repeat each pattern after the teacher reads it aloud, or listen to the track and follow the directions.
   (Key of G: Track 58; Key of F: Track 73)

② Think and then sing each pattern using solfege syllables.

③ Think and then sing each pattern using solfege syllables while fingering.

④ Think and then play each pattern.

# *Familiar Songs*

## G = do

### 17. Let Us Chase the Squirrel

*North Carolina*

Let us chase the squir - rel, Up the hick' - ry down the hick' - ry.

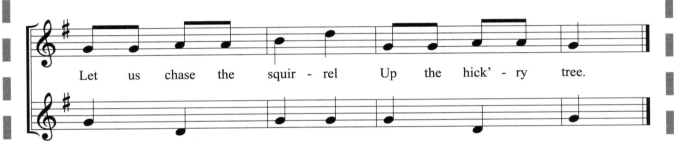

Let us chase the squir - rel Up the hick' - ry tree.

### 18. I Have a Dog

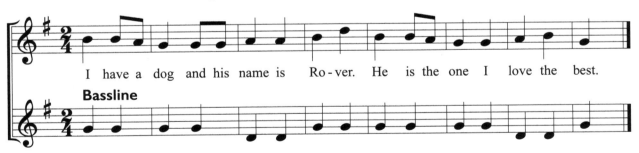

I have a dog and his name is Ro - ver. He is the one I love the best.

# Familiar Songs

## F = do

### 19.  Let Us Chase the Squirrel

*North Carolina**

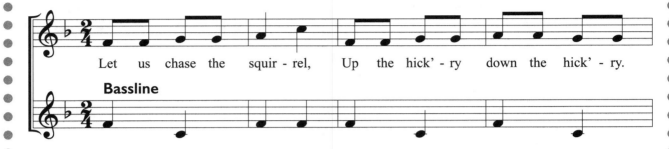

Let us chase the squir - rel, Up the hick' - ry down the hick' - ry.

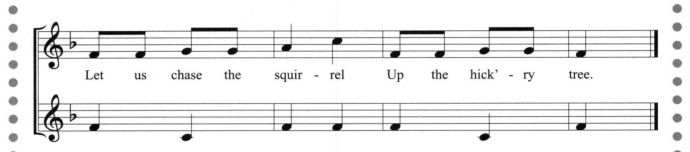

Let us chase the squir - rel Up the hick' - ry tree.

### 20.  I Have a Dog

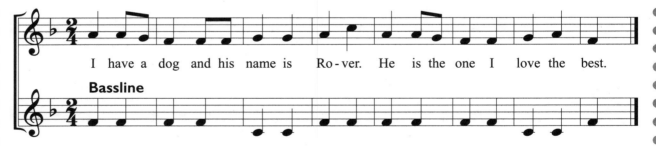

I have a dog and his name is Ro - ver. He is the one I love the best.

# Patterns Set 5D

1. Repeat each pattern after the teacher reads it aloud, or listen to the track and follow the directions.
   (Key of G: Track 59; Key of F: Track 74)

2. Think and then sing each pattern using solfege syllables.

3. Think and then sing each pattern using solfege syllables while fingering.

4. Think and then play each pattern.

# *Familiar Songs*

## *G = do*

### 21.  *Knock at the Door*

Knock at the door! Peep in! Pull the latch and walk in!

Bassline

### 22.  *Johnny Works with One Hammer*

John - ny works with one ham - mer, One ham - mer, one ham - mer.

Bassline

John - ny works with one ham - mer, Then he works with two.

# Familiar Songs

## F = do

### 23. Knock at the Door

Knock at the door! Peep in! Pull the latch and walk in!

**Bassline**

### 24. Johnny Works with One Hammer

John - ny works with one ham - mer, One ham - mer, one ham - mer.

**Bassline**

John - ny works with one ham - mer, Then he works with two.

# Patterns Set 5B

## G = do

1.

2.

3.

4.

5.

6.

7.

8.

## F = do

1.

2.

3.

4.

5.

6.

7.

8.

① Think and then sing each pattern using solfege syllables.

② Think and then sing each pattern using solfege syllables while fingering.

③ Think and then play each pattern.

44

# Unfamiliar Songs

## G = do

### 25. Go to Sleep

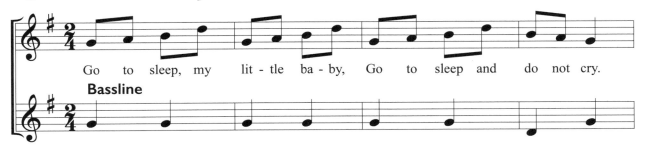

Go to sleep, my lit - tle ba - by, Go to sleep and do not cry.

**Bassline**

Moth - er's arms will hold you gent - ly while she sings a lul - la - by.

### 26. Fooba Wooba

Saw a flea kick a tree, Foo - ba, woo - ba, foo - ba, woo - ba.

**Bassline**

Saw a flea kick a tree, Foo - ba, woo - ba, John.

# *Unfamiliar Songs*

## *G = do (continued)*

### 27.  *Bells in the Steeple*

Bells in the stee-ple, So gai-ly do ring. This is a hol-i-day, Ding, ding, dong, ding.

### 28.  *Lady Bug*

*Czech and English*

La - dy - bug, La - dy - bug, fly a - way home. Your

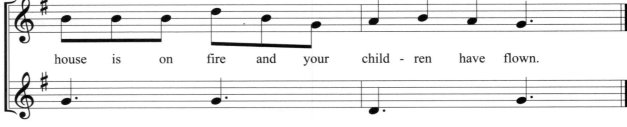

house is on fire and your child - ren have flown.

# Unfamiliar Songs

## F = do

### 29. Go to Sleep

Go to sleep, my lit - tle ba - by, Go to sleep and do not cry.

**Bassline**

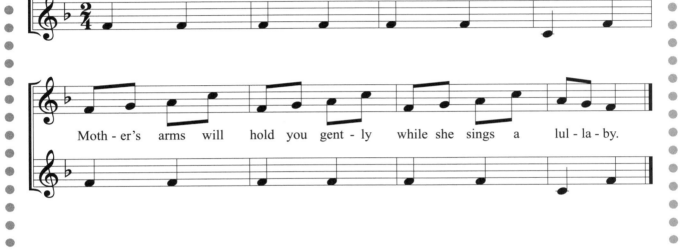

Moth - er's arms will hold you gent - ly while she sings a lul - la - by.

### 30. Fooba Wooba

Saw a flea kick a tree, Foo - ba, woo - ba, foo - ba, woo - ba.

**Bassline**

Saw a flea kick a tree, Foo - ba, woo - ba, John.

# F = do (continued)

## 31. Bells in the Steeple

Bells in the stee-ple, So gai-ly do ring.  This is a hol-i-day, Ding, ding, dong, ding.

**Bassline**

## 32. Lady Bug

*Czech and English*

La - dy - bug,  La - dy - bug,  fly  a - way  home.  Your

**Bassline**

house  is  on  fire  and  your  child - ren  have  flown.

# UNIT 6

# Guided Practice Activities
## Unit 6

Step 1: Readiness—Rote: All Around the Buttercup (F)                    _____Track 85

Step 1: Readiness—Rote: Swing a Lady Uptown (G)                        _____Track 86

Step 2: Conversational Solfege—Rote: Patterns 6A                       _____Track 87

Step 3: Conversational Solfege—Decode/Familiar: Patterns 6A           _____Track 88

Step 3: Conversational Solfege—Decode/Familiar: All Around the Buttercup (F)   _____Track 89

Step 3: Conversational Solfege—Decode/Familiar: Swing a Lady Uptown (G)        _____Track 90

Step 4: Conversational Solfege—Decode/Unfamiliar: Patterns 6B         _____Track 91

Step 4: Conversational Solfege—Decode/Unfamiliar: Try, Try Again (F)  _____Track 92

Step 4: Conversational Solfege—Decode/Unfamiliar: Grandma Grunts (G)  _____Track 93

Step 5: Conversational Solfege—Create                                 _____Track 94

*Complete all steps on this checklist with the voice first followed by recorder. Then proceed to the next page.*

# Patterns Set 6A

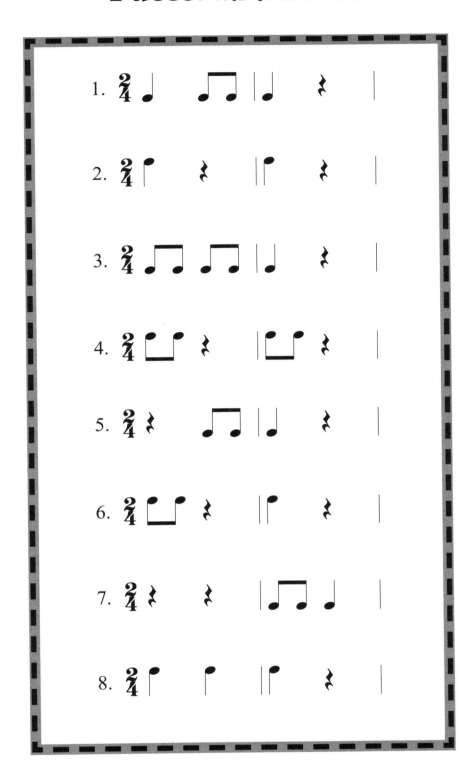

① Repeat each pattern after the teacher reads it aloud, or
listen to Track **87** and follow the directions.

② Think and then speak each pattern using rhythm syllables.

③ Think and then play each pattern on any pitch.

# Familiar Songs

### 33. All Around the Buttercup

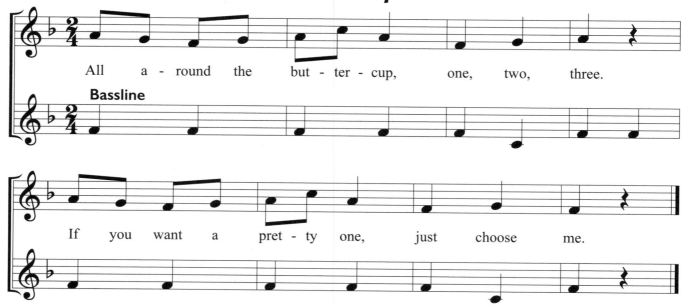

### 34. Swing a Lady Uptown

**African-American/
North Carolina**

### 35. Try, Try Again

**Feierabend**

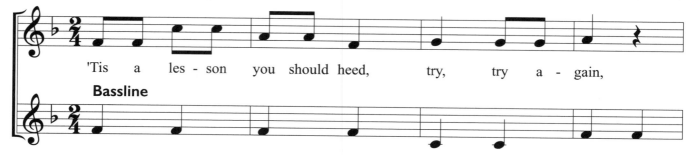

If at first you don't suc - ceed, try, try a - gain.

## 36. Grandma Grunts

**North Carolina**

Grand - ma Grunts said a cu - ri - ous thing,

**Bassline**

"Boys can whis - tle but girls must sing."

That is what I heard her say,

'Twas no long - er than yes - ter - day.

# Patterns Set 6B

① Think and then speak each pattern using rhythm syllables.

② Think and then play each pattern on any pitch.

# Unfamiliar Songs

## 37. I Have a Dog

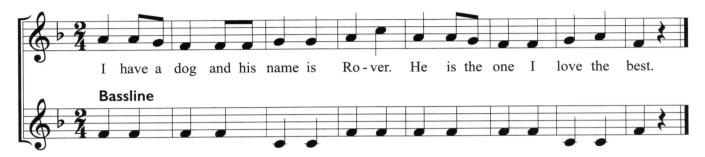

## 38. Let Us Chase the Squirrel

North Carolina

# UNIT 7

$$\frac{2}{4} \quad \natural$$

# *Guided Practice Activities*
## *Unit 7*

Step 1: Readiness—Rote: Pierott (F) _____Track 95

Step 1: Readiness—Rote: Pitter Patter (G) _____Track 96

Step 2: Conversational Solfege—Rote: Patterns 7A _____Track 97

Step 3: Conversational Solfege—Decode/Familiar: Patterns 7A _____Track 98

Step 3: Conversational Solfege—Decode/Familiar: Pierott (F) _____Track 99

Step 3: Conversational Solfege—Decode/Familiar: Pitter Patter (G) _____Track 100

Step 4: Conversational Solfege—Decode/Unfamiliar: Patterns 7B _____Track 101

Step 4: Conversational Solfege—Decode/Unfamiliar: Duerme, Duerme (F) _____Track 102

Step 4: Conversational Solfege—Decode/Unfamiliar: Bye Bye Baby (G) _____Track 103

Step 5: Conversational Solfege—Create _____Track 104

*Complete all steps on this checklist with the voice first followed by recorder. Then proceed to the next page.*

# Patterns Set 7A

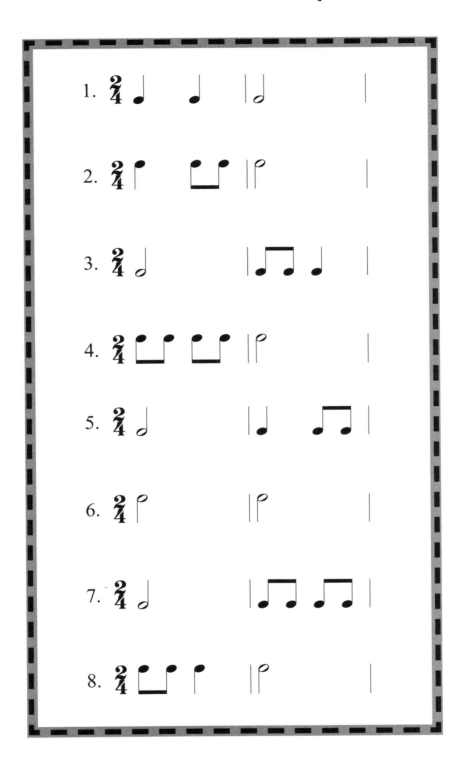

① Repeat each pattern after the teacher reads it aloud, or listen to Track **97** and follow the directions.

② Think and then speak each pattern using rhythm syllables.

③ Think and then play each pattern on any pitch.

# Familiar Songs

### 39. Pierott

French

Au Clair de la Lu - ne, Mon a - mi Pier - rot,
In the eve - ning moon - light stands Pier - rot to - night,

**Bassline**

Prè - tes - moi ta plu - me Pour é - crire un mot.
Plead - ing for a pen - cil so that he may write.

### 40. Pitter Patter

Pit - ter, pat - ter, Pit - ter, pat - ter, lis - ten to the rain.

**Bassline**

Pit - ter, pat - ter, Pit - ter, pat - ter, on my win - dow pane.

## 41. Duerme, Duerme

Spanish

Duer - me, duer - me, mu - ñe - qui - ta, duer - me ya.

**Bassline**

Si tu duer - mes tu ma - mi - ta dor - mir - á.

**General Translation:**

Sleep, sleep, my little one, go to sleep now.
If you sleep your mama will sleep too.

## 42. Bye Bye Baby

*Virginia*

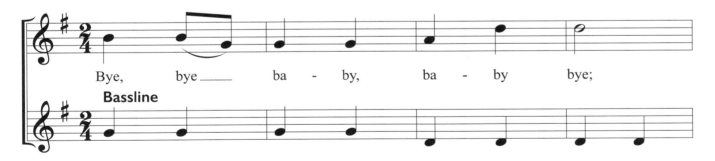

Bye, bye___ ba - by, ba - by bye;

**Bassline**

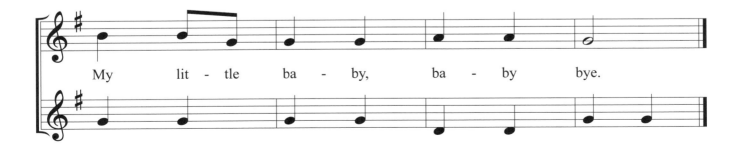

My lit - tle ba - by, ba - by bye.

# Patterns Set 7B

① Think and then speak each pattern using rhythm syllables.

② Think and then play each pattern on any pitch.

# Unfamiliar Songs

### 43. M'en Vais a Paris

French

M'en vais a Par - is sur un che - val gris.

**Bassline**

M'en vais a Tou - lous' sur un che - val rouge.

M'en vais a Tou - lon sur un vieux gri - son.

**General Translation:**

I am going to Paris on a gray horse.
I am going to Toulous' on a red horse.
I am going to Toulon on an old gray mare.

64

## 44. Sleep, Baby, Sleep

Sleep, ba - by, sleep. Fa - ther tends the sheep. Moth - er shakes the

**Bassline**

dream-land* tree and down come all the dreams for me. Sleep, ba - by, sleep.

**Original German Text:**

Schlaf, Kindlein, schlaf,
Der Vater hüt die Schaaf,
Die Mutter schüttelts Bäumelein,
Da fällt herab ein Träumelein,
Schlaf, Kindlein, schlaf.

*Also seen as apple tree.*

# UNIT 8

# Guided Practice Activities
## Unit 8

Step 1: Readiness–Rote: I'm a Little Dutch Girl (F) _____Track 105

Step 1: Readiness–Rote: Johnny Works with One Hammer (G) _____Track 106

Step 2: Conversational Solfege–Rote: Patterns 8A _____Track 107

Step 3: Conversational Solfege–Decode/Familiar: Patterns 8A _____Track 108

Step 3: Conversational Solfege–Decode/Familiar: I'm a Little Dutch Girl (F) _____Track 109

Step 3: Conversational Solfege–Decode/Familiar: Johnny Works with One Hammer (G) _____Track 110

Step 4: Conversational Solfege–Decode/Unfamiliar: Patterns 8B _____Track 111

Step 4: Conversational Solfege–Decode/Unfamiliar: Gathering Nuts (F) _____Track 112

Step 4: Conversational Solfege–Decode/Unfamiliar: Winter Will Be Here Soon (G) _____Track 113

Step 5: Conversational Solfege–Create _____Track 114

*Complete all steps on this checklist with the voice first followed by recorder. Then proceed to the next page.*

# Patterns Set 8A

① Repeat each pattern after the teacher reads it aloud, or listen to Track 107 and follow the directions.

② Think and then speak each pattern using rhythm syllables.

③ Think and then play each pattern on any pitch.

# Familiar Songs

## 45. I'm a Little Dutch Girl

## 46. Johnny Works with One Hammer

# Jingle Bells

Short version
Duet for soprano and alto recorder

Recorder Duet
by Kyle Coughlin

music and lyrics by
James Pierpont

69

## 47. Gathering Nuts

Feierabend

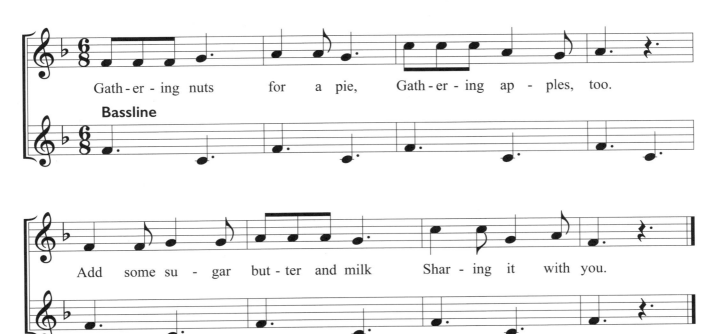

Gath - er - ing nuts for a pie, Gath - er - ing ap - ples, too.

**Bassline**

Add some su - gar but - ter and milk Shar - ing it with you.

## 48. Winter Will Be Here Soon

Feierabend

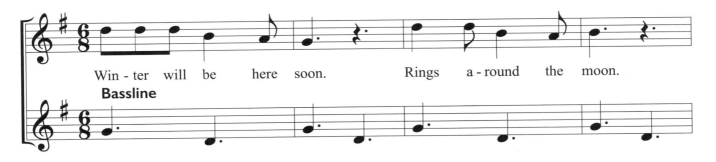

Win - ter will be here soon. Rings a - round the moon.

**Bassline**

Leaves are blow - ing through the air; Win - ter will be here soon.

# Patterns Set 8B

① Think and then speak each pattern using rhythm syllables.

② Think and then play each pattern on any pitch.

# UNIT 9

$$\frac{6}{8} \quad \textd{.}$$

# *Guided Practice Activities*
## *Unit 9*

Step 1: Readiness–Rote: Sailing (F)                                             _____Track 115

Step 1: Readiness–Rote: Setting the Sails (G)                                   _____Track 116

Step 2: Conversational Solfege–Rote: Patterns 9A                                _____Track 117

Step 3: Conversational Solfege–Decode/Familiar: Patterns 9A                     _____Track 118

Step 3: Conversational Solfege–Decode/Familiar: Sailing (F)                     _____Track 119

Step 3: Conversational Solfege–Decode/Familiar: Setting the Sails (G)           _____Track 120

Step 4: Conversational Solfege–Decode/Unfamiliar: Patterns 9B                   _____Track 121

Step 4: Conversational Solfege–Decode/Unfamiliar: Watching the Clouds (F)       _____Track 122

Step 4: Conversational Solfege–Decode/Unfamiliar: Red Bird (G)                  _____Track 123

Step 5: Conversational Solfege–Create                                          _____Track 124

*Complete all steps on this checklist with the voice first followed by recorder. Then proceed to the next page.*

# Patterns Set 9A

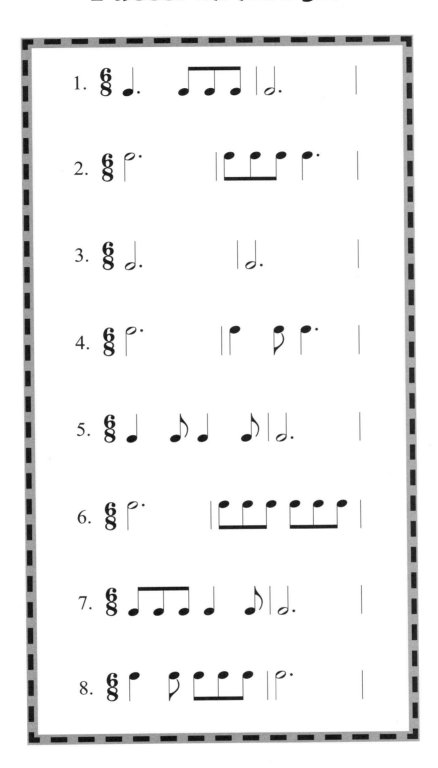

① Repeat each pattern after the teacher reads it aloud, or listen to Track 117 and follow the directions.

② Think and then speak each pattern using rhythm syllables.

③ Think and then play each pattern on any pitch.

# *Familiar Songs*

**PARTNER SONGS IN G**

## 49. *Sailing*

*Feierabend*

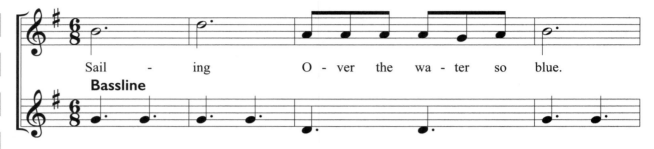

Sail - ing    O - ver the wa - ter so blue.

**Bassline**

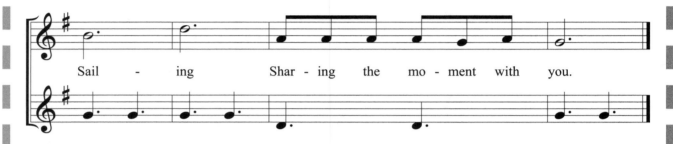

Sail - ing    Shar - ing the mo - ment with you.

## 50. *Setting the Sails*

*Feierabend*

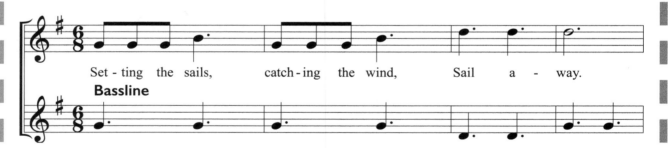

Set - ting the sails, catch - ing the wind, Sail a - way.

**Bassline**

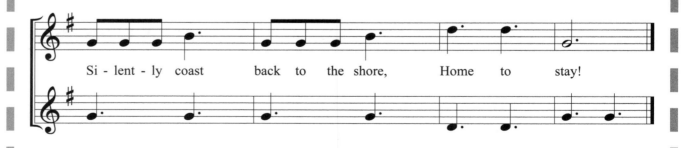

Si - lent - ly coast    back to the shore, Home to stay!

# *Familiar Songs*

## PARTNER SONGS IN F

### 51. *Sailing*

*Feierabend*

Sail - ing    O - ver the wa - ter so blue.

**Bassline**

Sail - ing    Shar - ing the mo - ment with you.

### 52. *Setting the Sails*

*Feierabend*

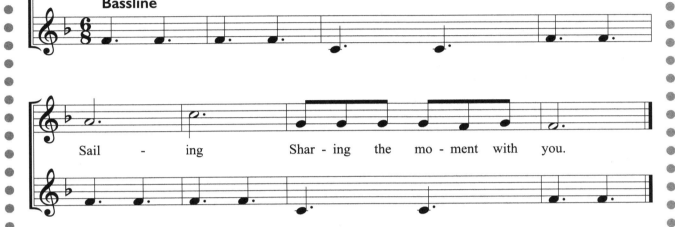

Set - ting the sails,    catch-ing the wind,    Sail a - way.

**Bassline**

Si - lent - ly coast    back to the shore,    Home to stay!

## 53. Watching the Clouds

Feierabend

Ly - ing here and look - ing up, Chang - ing shapes in the sky.

**Bassline**

Here's a horse and there's a goat. Watch-ing the clouds roll by.

## 54. Red Bird

Feierabend

Red Bird, Red Bird, Sit - ting in the tree.

**Bassline**

Red Bird, Red Bird, Won't you sing for me?

# Patterns Set 9B

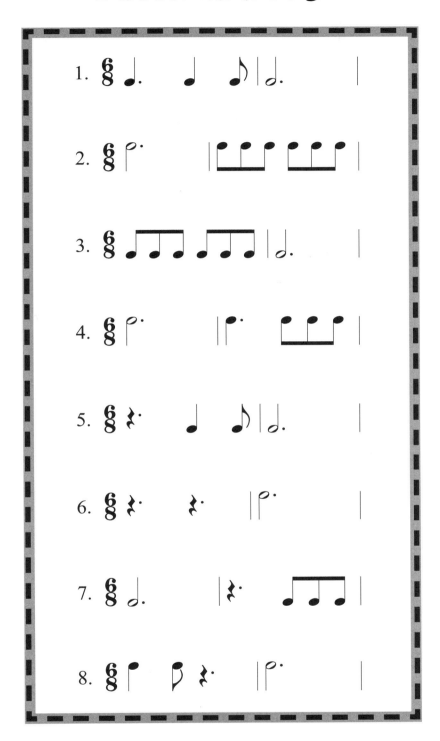

① Think and then speak each pattern using rhythm syllables.

② Think and then play each pattern on any pitch.

# UNIT 10

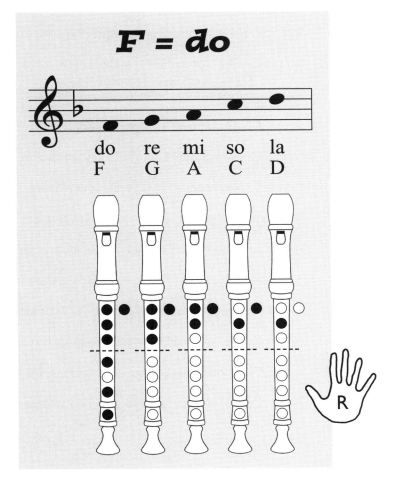

# Guided Practice Activities
## Unit 10

Step 1: Readiness—Rote: Bow Wow Wow (F) _____Track 125

Step 1: Readiness—Rote: Lonesome Dove (G) _____Track 126

Step 2: Conversational Solfege—Rote: Patterns 10A (F) _____Track 127

Step 2: Conversational Solfege—Rote: Patterns 10A (G) _____Track 128

Step 2: Conversational Solfege—Rote: Patterns 10C, #1–4 (F) _____Track 129

Step 2: Conversational Solfege—Rote: Patterns 10C, #5–8 (G) _____Track 130

Step 2: Conversational Solfege—Rote: Patterns 10D, #1–4 (F) _____Track 131

Step 2: Conversational Solfege—Rote: Patterns 10D, #5–8 (G) _____Track 132

Step 3: Conversational Solfege—Decode/Familiar: Patterns 10A (F) _____Track 133

Step 3: Conversational Solfege—Decode/Familiar: Patterns 10C (F) _____Track 134

Step 3: Conversational Solfege—Decode/Familiar: Bow Wow Wow (F) _____Track 135

Step 3: Conversational Solfege—Decode/Familiar: Patterns 10A (G) _____Track 136

Step 3: Conversational Solfege—Decode/Familiar: Patterns 10D (G) _____Track 137

Step 3: Conversational Solfege—Decode/Familiar: Lonesome Dove (G) _____Track 138

Step 4: Conversational Solfege—Decode/Unfamiliar: Patterns 10B, #1–4 (F) _____Track 139

Step 4: Conversational Solfege—Decode/Unfamiliar: Great Big House (F) _____Track 140

Step 4: Conversational Solfege-Decode/Unfamiliar: Patterns 10B, #5–8 (G) _____Track 141

Step 4: Conversational Solfege—Decode/Unfamiliar: Skinnymalink (G) _____Track 142

Step 5: Conversational Solfege—Create: Patterns in 2/4 (F) _____Track 143

Step 5: Conversational Solfege—Create: Patterns in 2/4 (G) _____Track 144

Step 5: Conversational Solfege—Create: Patterns in 6/8 (F) _____Track 145

Step 5: Conversational Solfege—Create: Patterns in 6/8 (G) _____Track 146

*Complete all steps on this checklist with the voice first followed by recorder. Then proceed to the next page.*

# Patterns Set 10A

## G = do

## F = do

① Repeat each pattern after the teacher reads it aloud, or listen to the track and follow the directions.
(Key of G: Track 128; Key of F: Track 127)

② Think and then sing each pattern using solfege syllables.

③ Think and then sing each pattern using solfege syllables while fingering.

④ Think and then play each pattern.

# Patterns Set 10C

① Repeat each pattern after the teacher reads it aloud, or listen to the track and follow the directions.
   (Key of G, Patterns 5–8: Track 130; Key of F, Patterns 1–4: Track 129)

② Think and then sing each pattern using solfege syllables.

③ Think and then sing each pattern using solfege syllables while fingering.

④ Think and then play each pattern.

# Familiar Songs

## 55. Bow Wow Wow

Bow, wow, wow, Whose dog art thou?

Bassline

Lit - tle Tom - my Tuck - er's dog. Bow, wow, wow.

## 56. Great Big House

African-American/Ohio

Great big house in New Or - leans, for - ty sto - ries high.____

Bassline

Ev - 'ry room that I've been in, 's filled with pump - kin* pie.

\* *Some versions use chicken pie.*

# *Patterns Set 10D*

### G = do

1.
2.
3.
4.
5.
6.
7.
8.

### F = do

1.
2.
3.
4.
5.
6.
7.
8.

① Repeat each pattern after the teacher reads it aloud, or listen to the track and follow the directions.
(Key of G, Patterns 5–8: Track 132; Key of F, Patterns 1–4: Track 131)

② Think and then sing each pattern using solfege syllables.

③ Think and then sing each pattern using solfege syllables while fingering.

④ Think and then play each pattern.

# Familiar Songs

## 57. Lonesome Dove

Tennessee

Down in some lone - some, pine - y grove,

**Bassline**

Down in some lone - some, pine - y grove,

Down in some lone - some, pine - y grove,

My lit - tle dove, she sits and moans.

## 58. Skinnymalink

*Irish*

Skin - ny - ma - link  me - lo - d'on legs,  Big ba - na - na feet.

**Bassline**

Went  to  the  pic - ture show,  But  could - n't  get  a  seat.

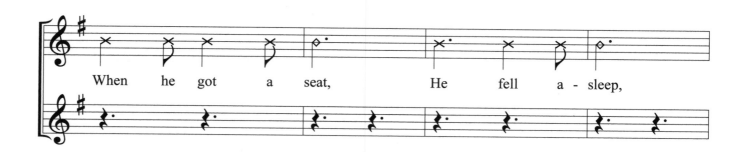

When  he  got  a  seat,  He  fell  a - sleep,

Skin - ny - ma - link  me - lo - d'on legs,  Big ba - na - na feet.

# Patterns Set 10B

## G = do

1.
2.
3.
4.
5.
6.
7.
8.

## F = do

1.
2.
3.
4.
5.
6.

① Think and then sing each pattern using solfege syllables.

② Think and then sing each pattern using solfege syllables while fingering.

③ Think and then play each pattern.

# *Unfamiliar Songs*

## 59. **Deta, Deta**

*Japanese*

De - ta, de - ta tsu - ki ga,

**Bassline**

Ma - ru - i, ma - ru - i man - ma - ru - i,

Bon _____ no yo na tsu - ki ga.

> **General Translation:**
>
> Rising, rising is the moon,
> Large and round, large and round, round round one,
> Plate-like full moon will rise soon.

## 60. **Rocky Mountain**

Rock - y moun - tain, rock - y moun - tain, rock - y moun - tain high.

**Bassline**

When you're on that rock-y moun-tain, hang your head and cry!

Do, do, do, do, do re - mem - ber me.

Do, do, do, do, do re - mem - ber me.

## 61. Ickle Ockle

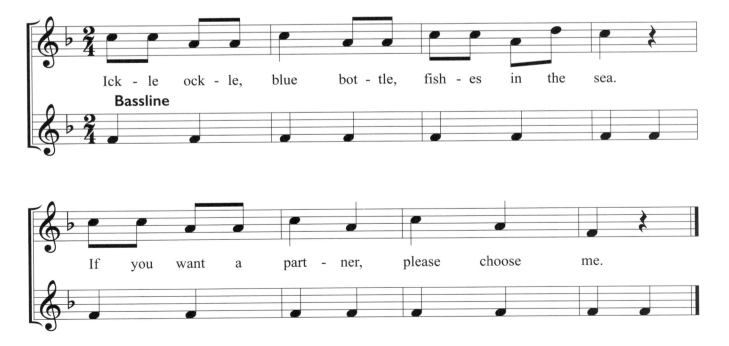

Ick - le ock - le, blue bot - tle, fish - es in the sea.

**Bassline**

If you want a part - ner, please choose me.

90

## 62. *Button You Must Wander*

But - ton you must wan - der, wan - der, wan - der,

**Bassline**

But - ton you must wan - der far a - way.

Bright eyes will find you. Sharp eyes will find you.

But - ton you must wan - der ev'ry - where.

### 63. Button Trio for Instruments — Arr. John Feierabend

Bassline

## 64. Sally Go 'Round the Sun

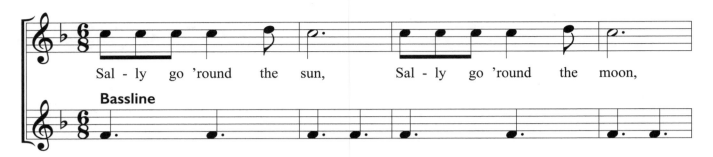

Sal - ly go 'round the sun, Sal - ly go 'round the moon,

**Bassline**

Sal - ly go 'round the chim - ney pot, Ev - 'ry af - ter - noon.

# UNIT 11

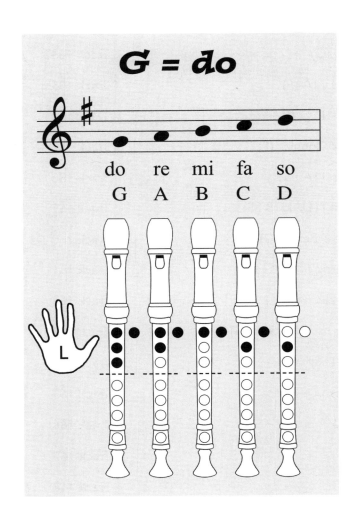

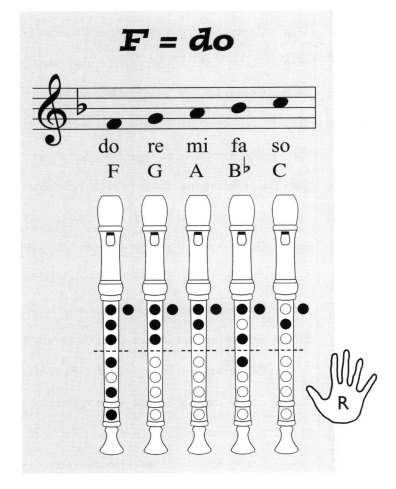

# *Guided Practice Activities*
## *Unit 11*

Step 1: Readiness—Rote: Cobbler Cobbler (F)                                 _____Track 147

Step 1: Readiness—Rote: Oat Peas Beans (G)                                 _____Track 148

Step 2: Conversational Solfege—Rote: Patterns 11A (F)                     _____Track 149

Step 2: Conversational Solfege—Rote: Patterns 11A (G)                     _____Track 150

Step 2: Conversational Solfege—Rote: Patterns 11C, #1–4 (F)              _____Track 151

Step 2: Conversational Solfege—Rote: Patterns 11C, #5–8 (G)              _____Track 152

Step 2: Conversational Solfege—Rote: Patterns 11D, #1–4 (F)              _____Track 153

Step 2: Conversational Solfege—Rote: Patterns 11D, #5–8 (G)              _____Track 154

Step 3: Conversational Solfege—Decode/Familiar: Patterns 11A (F)         _____Track 155

Step 3: Conversational Solfege—Decode/Familiar: Patterns 11C, #1–4 (F)   _____Track 156

Step 3: Conversational Solfege—Decode/Familiar: Cobbler Cobbler (F)      _____Track 157

Step 3: Conversational Solfege—Decode/Familiar: Patterns 11A (G)         _____Track 158

Step 3: Conversational Solfege—Decode/Familiar: Patterns 11D, #5–8 (G)   _____Track 159

Step 3: Conversational Solfege—Decode/Familiar: Oats Peas Beans (G)      _____Track 160

Step 4: Conversational Solfege—Decode/Unfamiliar: Patterns 11B, #1–4 (F) _____Track 161

Step 4: Conversational Solfege—Decode/Unfamiliar: One Elephant (F)       _____Track 162

Step 4: Conversational Solfege—Decode/Unfamiliar: Patterns 11B, #5–8 (G) _____Track 163

Step 4: Conversational Solfege—Decode/Unfamiliar: Lady Lady (G)          _____Track 164

Step 5: Conversational Solfege—Create: Patterns in 2/4 (F)               _____Track 165

Step 5: Conversational Solfege—Create: Patterns in 2/4 (G)               _____Track 166

Step 5: Conversational Solfege—Create: Patterns in 6/8 (F)               _____Track 167

Step 5: Conversational Solfege—Create: Patterns in 6/8 (G)               _____Track 168

*Complete all steps on this checklist with the voice first followed by recorder. Then proceed to the next page.*

# Patterns Set 11A

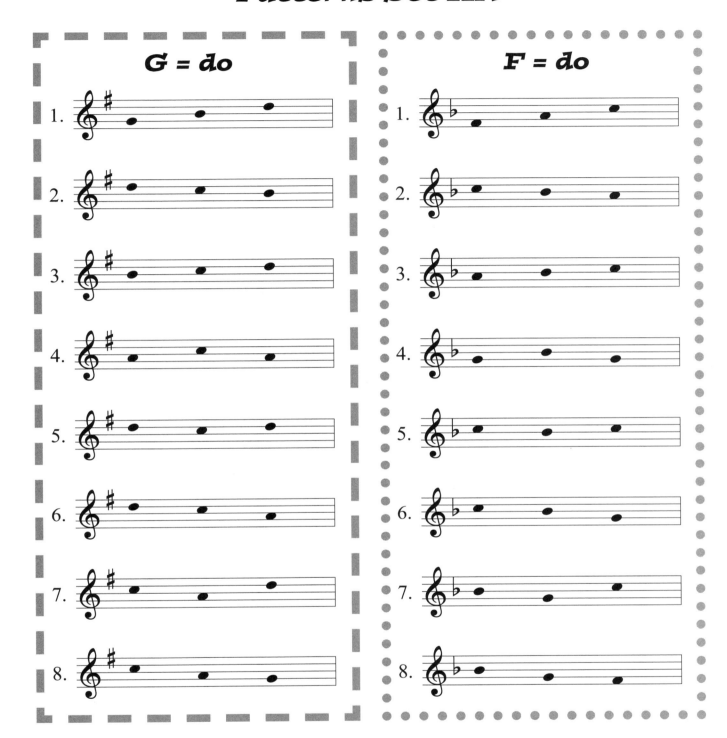

① Repeat each pattern after the teacher reads it aloud, or listen to the track and follow the directions.
(Key of G: Track 150; Key of F: Track 149)

② Think and then sing each pattern using solfege syllables.

③ Think and then sing each pattern using solfege syllables while fingering.

④ Think and then play each pattern.

# Patterns Set 11C

① Repeat each pattern after the teacher reads it aloud, or listen to the track and follow the directions. (Key of G, Patterns 5–8: Track 152; Key of F, Patterns 1–4: Track 151)

② Think and then sing each pattern using solfege syllables.

③ Think and then sing each pattern using solfege syllables while fingering.

④ Think and then play each pattern.

# Familiar Songs

## 65. Cobbler Cobbler

Cob - bler, cob - bler, mend my shoe. Have it done by half past two.

Tu - ra - lu - ra - lu. Half past two is much too late,

Have it done by half past eight. Tu - ra - lu - ra - lu.

## 66. One Elephant

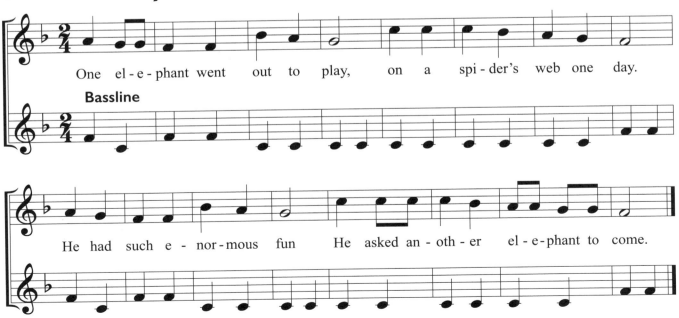

One el - e - phant went out to play, on a spi - der's web one day.

He had such e - nor - mous fun He asked an - oth - er el - e - phant to come.

98

# Patterns Set 11D

① Repeat each pattern after the teacher reads it aloud, or listen to the track and follow the directions.
(Key of G, Patterns 5–8: Track 154; Key of F, Patterns 1–4: Track 153)

② Think and then sing each pattern using solfege syllables.

③ Think and then sing each pattern using solfege syllables while fingering.

④ Think and then play each pattern.

# Familiar Songs

## 67. Oats Peas Beans

*European*

Oats, peas, beans and bar - ley grow. Oats, peas, beans and bar - ley grow. Do

**Bassline**

you or I or an - y - one know how oats, peas, beans and bar - ley grow?

## 68. Lady Lady

La - dy, La - dy, Buy a broom for my ba - by.

**Bassline**

Sweep it low, sweep it high, Sweep the cob - webs out of the sky.

La - dy, La - dy, Buy a broom for my ba - by.

# Patterns Set 11B

**G = do**

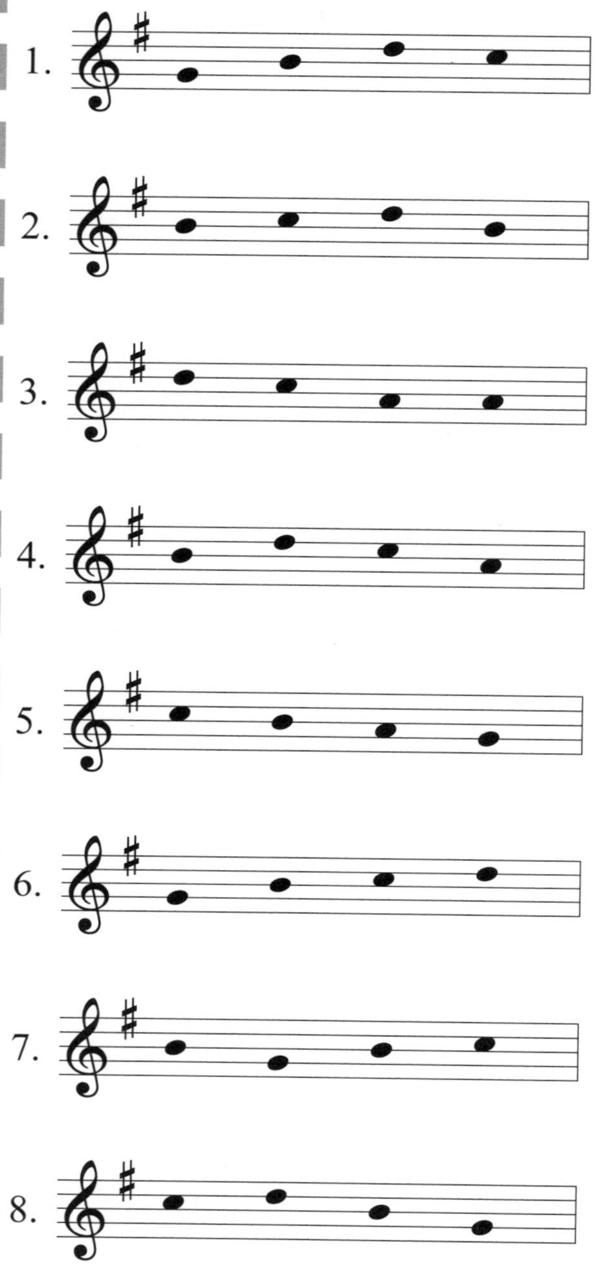

**F = do**

① Think and then sing each pattern using solfege syllables.

② Think and then sing each pattern using solfege syllables while fingering.

③ Think and then play each pattern.

# *Unfamiliar Songs*

## 69. *Hidi Hidi-Ho*

102

## 70. Wishy Washy

Oh, we are two sail - ors late - ly come from sea, ___ And

if you want an - oth - er one, come a - long with me. Oh,

wish - y wash - y, wish - y wash - y, wish - y wash - y wee, ___ And

if you want an - oth - er one, come a - long with me.

## 71. Dodo, l'enfant Dors

**French**

*Do - do, l'en - fant dors, l'en - fant dor - mi - ra bien vi - te.*
Sleep, ___ ba - by sleep, ba - by go to sleep quite quick - ly.

**72. Go Tell Aunt Rhody**

*African-American/*
*South Carolina*

## 73. Lightly Row

Light - ly row, Light - ly row, o'er the glass - y waves we go;

Bassline

Smooth - ly glide, smooth - ly glide, on the si - lent tide.

Let the winds and wa - ters be min - gled with our mel - o - dy;

Sing and float, sing and float, in our lit - tle boat.

104

## 74. Lullaby

Canadian

Lul - la - by, lul - la - by. Do not wake and weep.

Soft - ly in the cra - dle lie, sleep, o sleep!

Soft - ly in the cra - dle lie, sleep, my dar - ling, sleep.

## 75. Now the Day Is Over

Barnby (1867)

## 76. Ambos A Dos

Puerto Rico

**77. Wind the Bobbin** English

## 78. Barcarolle

Italian, arr. Offenbach*

## 79. Workin' on the Railroad

Alan Lomax/
Library of Congress

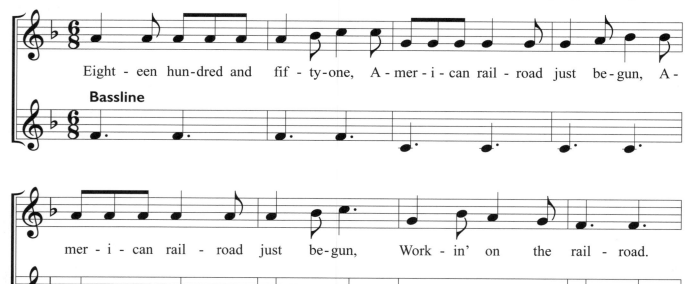

Eight - een hun-dred and fif - ty-one, A - mer - i - can rail - road just be-gun, A -

Bassline

mer - i - can rail - road just be-gun, Work - in' on the rail - road.

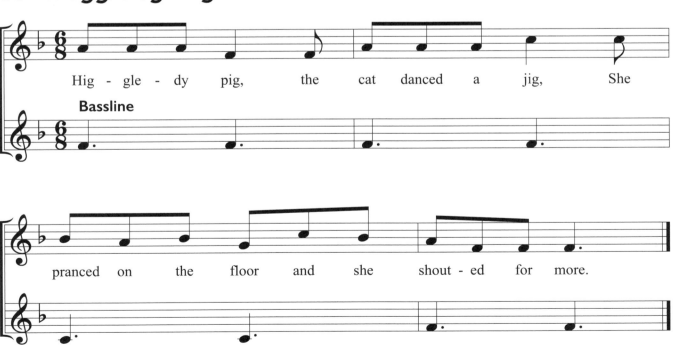

**Chorus**

Pat - sy o - ree - o - ree - ay, Pat - sy o - ree - o - ree - ay. Oh,

Pat - sy o - ree - o - ree - ay, Work - in' on the rail - road.

## 80. Higgledy Pig

Hig - gle - dy pig, the cat danced a jig, She

**Bassline**

pranced on the floor and she shout - ed for more.

## 81. Hippety Hop to the Candy Shop

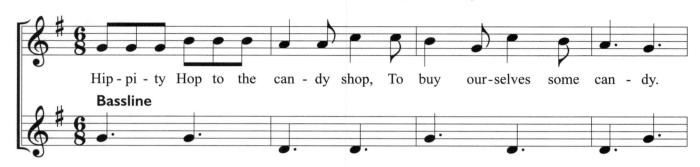

Hip-pi-ty Hop to the can-dy shop, To buy our-selves some can-dy.

**Bassline**

Some for you and some for me, And some for sis - ter Man - dy.

# UNIT 12

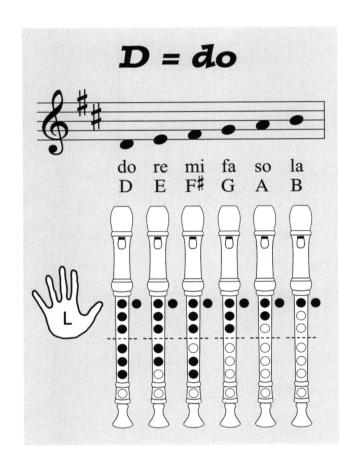

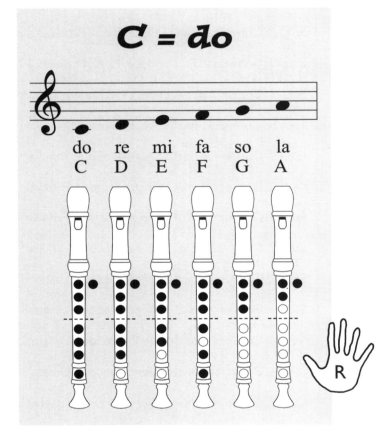

# *Guided Practice Activities*
## *Unit 12*

Step 1: Readiness–Rote: Obwisana (D) _____Track 169

Step 1: Readiness–Rote: O, How Lovely (C) _____Track 170

Step 2: Conversational Solfege–Rote: Patterns 12A (D) _____Track 171

Step 2: Conversational Solfege–Rote: Patterns 12A (C) _____Track 172

Step 2: Conversational Solfege–Rote: Patterns 12C, #1–4 (D) _____Track 173

Step 2: Conversational Solfege–Rote: Patterns 12C, #5–8 (C) _____Track 174

Step 2: Conversational Solfege–Rote: Patterns 12D, #1–4 (D) _____Track 175

Step 2: Conversational Solfege–Rote: Patterns 12D, #5–8 (C) _____Track 176

Step 3: Conversational Solfege–Decode/Familiar: Patterns 12A (D) _____Track 177

Step 3: Conversational Solfege–Decode/Familiar: Patterns 12C (D) _____Track 178

Step 3: Conversational Solfege–Decode/Familiar: Obwisana (D) _____Track 179

Step 3: Conversational Solfege–Decode/Familiar: Patterns 12A (C) _____Track 180

Step 3: Conversational Solfege–Decode/Familiar: Patterns 12D (C) _____Track 181

Step 3: Conversational Solfege–Decode/Familiar: O, How Lovely (C) _____Track 182

Step 4: Conversational Solfege–Decode/Unfamiliar: Patterns 12B (D) _____Track 183

Step 4: Conversational Solfege–Decode/Unfamiliar: Over in the Meadow (D) _____Track 184

Step 4: Conversational Solfege–Decode/Unfamiliar: Patterns 12B (C) _____Track 185

Step 4: Conversational Solfege–Decode/Unfamiliar: Looby Loo (C) _____Track 186

Step 5: Conversational Solfege–Create: Patterns in 2/4 (D) _____Track 187

Step 5: Conversational Solfege–Create: Patterns in 2/4 (C) _____Track 188

Step 5: Conversational Solfege–Create: Patterns in 6/8 (D) _____Track 189

Step 5: Conversational Solfege–Create: Patterns in 6/8 (C) _____Track 190

*Complete all steps on this checklist with the voice first followed by recorder. Then proceed to the next page.*

# Patterns Set 12A

**D = do**

1.
2.
3.
4.
5.
6.
7.
8.

**C = do**

1.
2.
3.
4.
5.
6.
7.
8.

① Repeat each pattern after the teacher reads it aloud, or listen to the track and follow the directions. (Key of D: Track 171; Key of C: Track 172)

② Think and then sing each pattern using solfege syllables.

③ Think and then sing each pattern using solfege syllables while fingering.

④ Think and then play each pattern.

# Patterns Set 12C

D = do

C = do

① Repeat each pattern after the teacher reads it aloud, or listen to the track and follow the directions.
(Key of D, Patterns 1–4: Track 173; Key of C, Patterns 5–8: Track 174)

② Think and then sing each pattern using solfege syllables.

③ Think and then sing each pattern using solfege syllables while fingering.

④ Think and then play each pattern.

# Familiar Songs

## 82. Obwisana

Ghanaian

Ob - wi - sa - na sa na - na, Ob - wi - sa - na sa.

**Bassline**

Ob - wi - sa - na sa na - na, Ob - wi - sa - na sa.

**General Translation:**

The rock has crushed my hand, grandma.

## 83. Over in the Meadow

O - ver in the mea - dow, in the sand in the sun, Lived an old moth - er tur - tle and her lit - tle tur - tle one. "Dig," said the moth - er, "I dig," said the one, So he dug and was glad in the sand in the sun.

Bassline

# Patterns Set 12D

## D = do

1.

2.

3.

4.

5.

6.

7.

8.

## C = do

1.

2.

3.

4.

5.

6.

7.

8.

① Repeat each pattern after the teacher reads it aloud, or listen to the track and follow the directions.
(Key of D, Patterns 1–4: Track 175; Key of C, Patterns 5–8: Track 176)

② Think and then sing each pattern using solfege syllables.

③ Think and then sing each pattern using solfege syllables while fingering.

④ Think and then play each pattern.

# Familiar Songs

## 84. O, How Lovely

**1.** O, how love-ly is the eve-ning, is the eve-ning;

**Bassline**

**2.** When the bells are sweet-ly ring-ing, sweet-ly ring-ing.

**3.** Ding Dong, Ding Dong, Ding Dong.

## 85. Looby Loo

*Scottish and English*

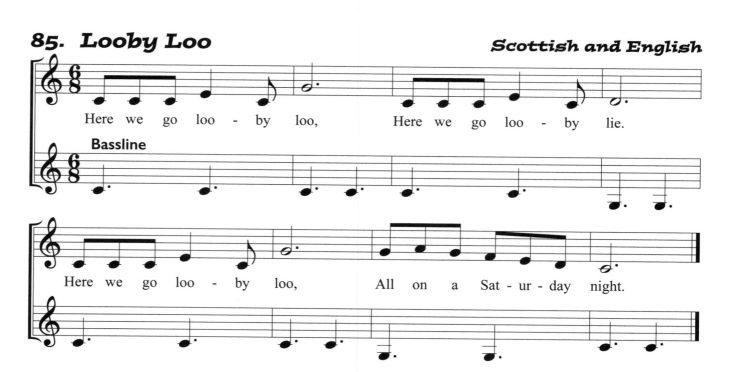

Here we go loo-by loo, Here we go loo-by lie.

**Bassline**

Here we go loo-by loo, All on a Sat-ur-day night.

# Patterns Set 12B

**D = do**

1.
2.
3.
4.
5.

**C = do**

1.
2.
3.
4.
5.
6.
7.
8.

① Think and then sing each pattern using solfege syllables.

② Think and then sing each pattern using solfege syllables while fingering.

③ Think and then play each pattern.

# Unfamiliar Songs

## 86. A Branch of May

I've been a-wan-d'ring all through this___ night and the best part of the day, But when I___ come back home a-gain, I will bring you a branch of ___ May.___

## 87. Bye, Oh My Baby

Bye, oh my ba - by, ba - by bye, oh, bye,

**Bassline**

Go to sleep, my hon - ey, Hon - ey bye, oh, bye.

Bye, oh my sug - ar, Sug - ar go to sleep,

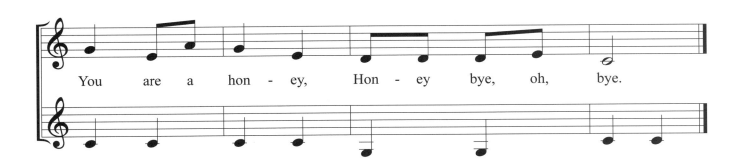

You are a hon - ey, Hon - ey bye, oh, bye.

## 88. Hob ich a por Oksn

Yiddish

Hob ich a por ok - sn, ok - sn, Vos zey bro - kn

**Bassline**

lok - shn, lok - shn, Ay, vun - der i - ber vun - der,

ay, vun - der i - ber vun - der, Vi di ok - sn bro - kn lok - shn,

Dos iz mir a vun - der, doz iz mir a vun - der.

**General Translation:**

I have a pair of oxen that chop noodles,
Ah! Wonder of wonders, how the oxen chop noodles,
What a wonder.

## 89. Ah! Vous Diraisje, Maman

French

**Bassline**

Ah! Vous di - rais - je, Ma - man, Ce que cau - se mon tour - ment!

Pa - pa veut que je rai - sonne, Com-me u - ne grande per - sonne;

Moi je dis que les bon - bons, Va - lent mieux que lo rai - son.

**General Translation:**

Oh! Shall I tell you, Mama, what is tormenting me?
Daddy wants me to reason like a grown-up person;
Me, I say that sweets are worth more than reasoning.

124

## 90. Alle Meine Entchen

German

**Bassline**

Al - le mei - ne Ent - chen schwim - men auf dem See, schwim - men auf dem See, Köpf - chen in das Was - ser, Schwänz - chen in die Höh'.

---

**General Translation:**

All my little ducklings swimming in the lake,
Heads dunk in the water, as little tails do shake.

## 91. Savez Vous Plantar des Choux?  French Canadian*

**General Translation:**

Do you know how to plant cabbage the way we do it?

## 92. 14th Century German Tune

### 93. Davey, Davey Dumpling

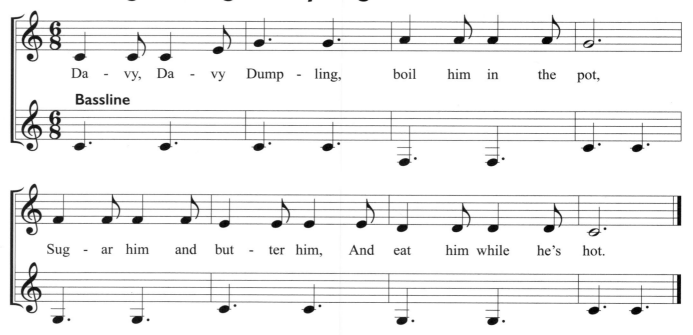

Da - vy, Da - vy Dump - ling, boil him in the pot,

Bassline

Sug - ar him and but - ter him, And eat him while he's hot.

### 94. Fiddle Dee-Dee

Fid - dle dee dee, fid - dle dee dee, the fly has mar - ried the bum - ble-bee. Said the

Bassline

fly, said he, "Will you mar - ry me? And live with me, sweet bum - ble - bee?"

Fid - dle dee dee, fid - dle dee dee, the fly has mar - ried the bum - ble-bee.

## 95. I Can Hammer

## 96. O Missis Sippy-o

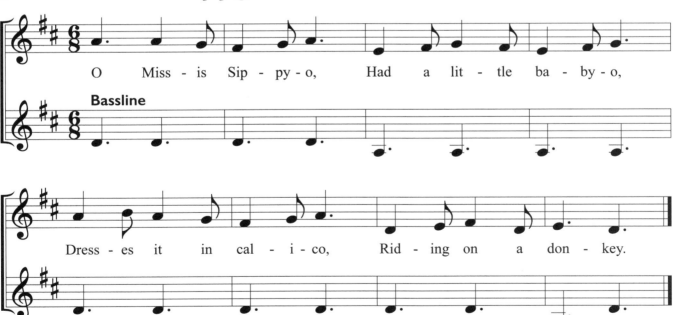

## 97. The Woodsman's Alphabet Song

Maine

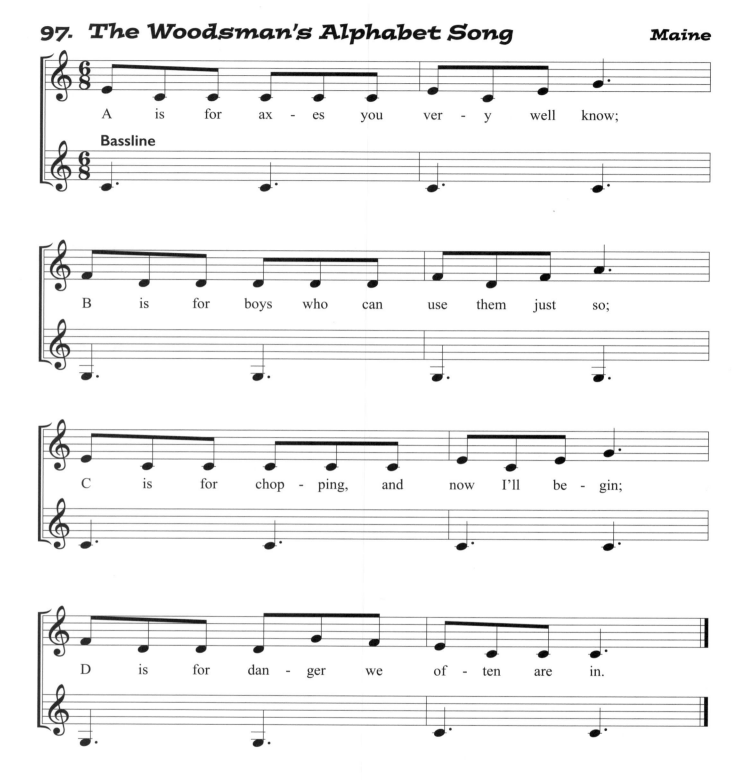

A is for ax - es you ver - y well know;

B is for boys who can use them just so;

C is for chop - ping, and now I'll be - gin;

D is for dan - ger we of - ten are in.

## 98. Do, Re, Mi

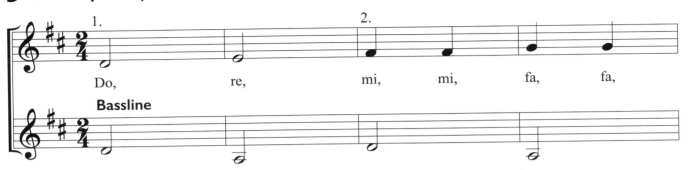

Do, re, mi, mi, fa, fa,

I am tired of this so-fa-ing And I know not what you're say-ing.

# UNIT 13

# *Guided Practice Activities*
## *Unit 13*

Step 1: Readiness—Rote: Red Sky at Night (D)                                        ____Track 191

Step 1: Readiness—Rote: Sleep Bonnie Barney (C)                                 ____Track 192

Step 2: Conversational Solfege—Rote: Patterns 13A                             ____Track 193

Step 3: Conversational Solfege—Decode/Familiar: Patterns 13A             ____Track 194

Step 3: Conversational Solfege—Decode/Familiar: Red Sky at Night (D)     ____Track 195

Step 3: Conversational Solfege—Decode/Familiar: Sleep Bonnie Barney (C)    ____Track 196

Step 4: Conversational Solfege—Decode/Unfamiliar: Patterns 13B            ____Track 197

Step 4: Conversational Solfege—Decode/Unfamiliar: One Man Went to Mow (D)    ____Track 198

Step 4: Conversational Solfege—Decode/Unfamiliar: Mister Fly Went Buzzing By (C)    ____Track 199

Step 5: Conversational Solfege—Create                                          ____Track 200

*Complete all steps on this checklist with the voice first followed by recorder. Then proceed to the next page.*

# Patterns Set 13A

① Repeat each pattern after the teacher reads it aloud, or
listen to Track 193 and follow the directions.

② Think and then speak each pattern using rhythm syllables.

③ Think and then play each pattern on any pitch.

# *Familiar Songs*

## *99. Red Sky at Night*

*Feierabend*

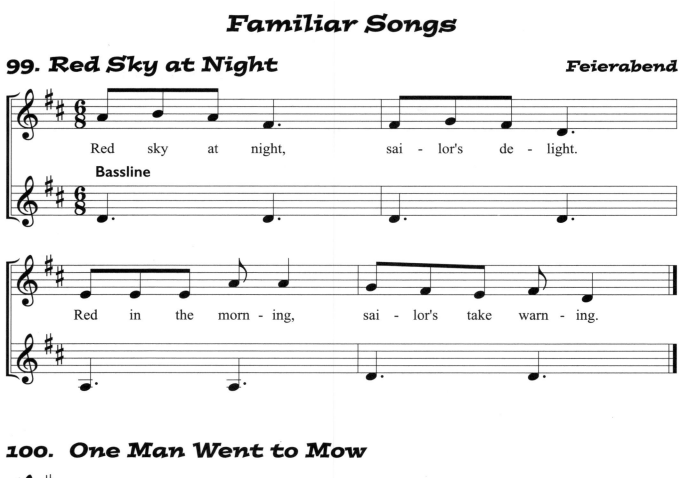

## *100. One Man Went to Mow*

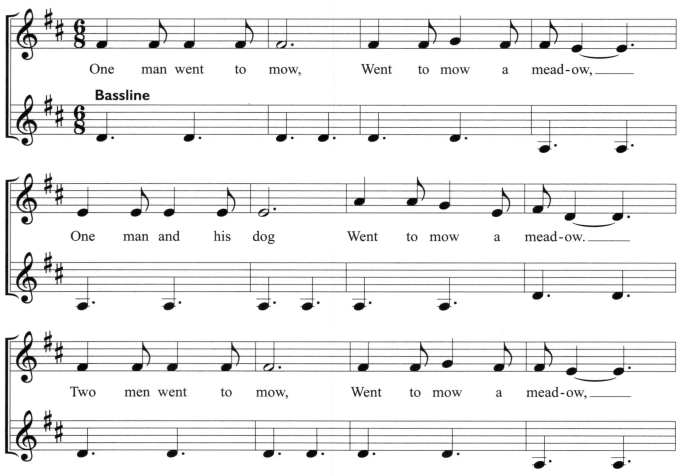

Two   men, one   man   and   his dog   Went   to   mow   a   mead-ow.

## 101. *Sleep Bonnie Barney*

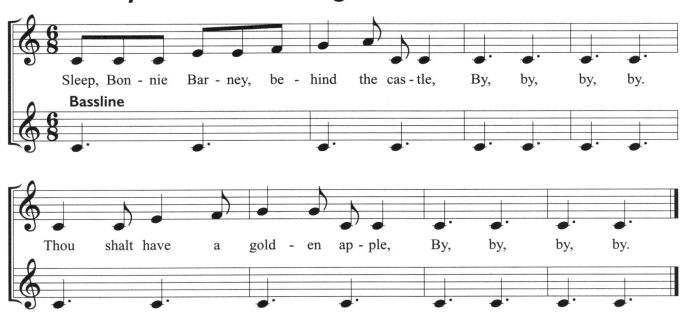

Sleep, Bon - nie  Bar - ney,  be - hind  the cas - tle,  By,  by,  by,  by.

**Bassline**

Thou   shalt have   a   gold - en   ap - ple,   By,   by,   by,   by.

## 102. *Mister Fly Went Buzzing By*          *Feierabend*

Mis - ter  Fly went   buz - zing by,   Mis - ter  Frog did   spy   him.

**Bassline**

Sud - den - ly  they   came  eye   to  eye,   Mis - ter  Fly's  fu - ture  was   dim.

# Patterns Set 13B

① Think and then speak each pattern using rhythm syllables.

② Think and then play each pattern on any pitch.